Mary Meriam is a rare and original poet. This is a dazzling book, a fusion of anguish and wit and song, written in clear and compelling language. I love the wildness, the inventiveness, the always surprising but accurate metaphors. She writes of real things, real people, always musically. She uses Mother Goose rhythms and rhymes or echoes of Sapphic meters or settings as grim as any of the Grimm Brothers' tales, to tell searing truths that move, frighten, and delight one with the skill of their telling.
—**Naomi Replansky**

Conjuring My Leafy Muse is, in numerous ways, a marvel of incantation and lyricism, a weaving of the supernatural, horrific, sensual, folkloric, and disarmingly frank. Mary Meriam's poetry has a haunting, genuine quality in which she combines the disturbing and profoundly disappointing aspects of life with a vivid, forthright nonchalance. She confesses her personal truths with unblinking sincerity. As we might infer from the title, she sometimes uses the rhythm of predetermined meter as if she were casting a spell, discovering for us and with us the exquisitely miraculous: a boiling pot of beans, a herd of deer, cottontail in clover. This is an intensely moving collection of poetry by a writer whose voice is fresh.
—*Foreword Reviews*

Mary Meriam is a frightening poet, a frighteningly good poet. The intensity of her writing will frighten you, but also her technical skill. She can put a chill into the most common rhyme. The poems speak like "a gust of gorgeous / thundering swallows." She identifies her models as Christina Rossetti and Charlotte Mew, whose Goblin Market and "Farmer's Bride" rightfully haunt the collection. But her real soulmate is Thomas Lovell Beddoes, the ultimate poet of the queer and scary whose masterpiece, *Death's Jest Book,* was left appropriately unfinished. She may ask us to "unspook" her dreams, but we won't succeed. The uncanny is too engrained in her sensibility. All we can ask is that she continue to keep writing.
—**David Bergman**

Mary Meriam is a poet who takes risks, by which I don't mean what you think I mean. There's nothing risky about breaking rules that haven't been in effect since 1880. I'm talking about the

modern rules, the new respectability, the advice given in poetry workshops by legions of successful poets whom no one reads. Mary doesn't give a shit about Pound's "don'ts," she's too busy writing fierce, gorgeous poems about love and pain. She's a true rebel, in all her heartfelt, singsong, vulnerable, girly glory.
— Rose Kelleher

Mary Meriam's new collection is a treasure chest of charm and trouble. Her sonnets, lyrics and chants show the best of the New Formalism, being personal but not ever inaccessibly private, and musical without a touch of pretense. There is life and sweetness in her approach, and reproach and rue as well.
— Zachary Bos

Mary Meriam is an accomplished technician and imaginative Mother Goose artist, who like Mother Goose (my favorite collection in the world), is almost always serious, even tragic, along with fun. I am floored by poems with lines like the opening of "I Learn Today My Mother Lied": *"Not one drop of Jewish blood / in me or you!" my mother cried, / as if she had a drop to hide...* We are lucky to have her dissident voice.
— Willis Barnstone

This is my kind of a poet. 'She speaks,' as Larkin said of the beautiful and wistful and utterly different Stevie Smith, 'with the authority of sadness.' She also speaks in the language of tradition. She uses old forms fiercely. She is rather a fierce poet. Oh, and a Lesbian. You can't ignore that. But what does she do? Do with words. Magic. Above all, Mary Meriam is a magic poet and if that is what you want (as I do) this is a book for you.
— John Whitworth

Mary Meriam doesn't flinch at female eroticism, at emotional turmoil, at social upheaval, at the truth of human cruelty. She also doesn't flinch at rhyme, rhythm, formal constraint, or ancient forms of poetry and language. Even the singsong breathes fire. Mother Goose taunts the guilty mothers. But no gratuitous haranguing here: these are gut poems, deeply felt, yet adeptly and sensitively composed. . . . And in the end, it is what rings true that endures. Because deeper truths are the most satisfying venue of poetry, the poet who incorporates beauty with horror, pain

with transformation, calm with the unsettling, love with human destruction, is the poet whom we will finally remember when the curtain falls and the kudos and snipes have been doled out. This trilogy, a comprehensive selection of her work, displays that more deeply satisfying yin-yang of poetry. Mary Meriam's poetry will not go away, and in this world of excess talent and uncountable literary stars, that is saying a lot.
—*Autostraddle*

Song is mysterious. It seems to arise when the separation between sophistication and simplicity has been submerged in deep water. Song is that ringing-out of the wrung heart whereby what is personal becomes what is universal—and so it is fitting that all the archetypal seasons in Mary Meriam's *Girlie Calendar* have their own specific songs to share, their own ardent delights. Yet these delights are hard-fought, because song is also that inspiring moment of transcendence so in evidence in the courage of these lines: *A knife of pain may bend you over double, / but hover, swing from your trapeze, breathe.* Mary Meriam's songs are thus both breath-taking and breath-giving. Indeed, there is a rigor of architecture in these poems, as well as in the construction of the book as a whole, that is exacting, deliberate, astonishingly disciplined—and yet surrendering to such songs, as a reader, seems as natural as breathing. *Let steel become a sigh,* she sings to herself in her month of August. Those five words rise and fall as an exquisitely fragile monument to all song. I would even go so far as to say that they are a powerful medicine for what ails us.
— **R. Nemo Hill**

Mary Meriam's formalist poems are compressed bliss, dreamlike couplets and velvet quatrains honed to a fabric delightfully carnal. Like two of her touchstones, Frost and Bishop, her masterful metrics are handmaidens to her message at play in the fields of passion, loss, and redemption.
— **J. Patrick Lewis**

This is very strong, fearless stuff, beautiful.
— **Rhina P. Espaillat**

Books by Mary Meriam

Full-Length Collections
Girlie Calendar
Conjuring My Leafy Muse

Chapbooks
The Lesbian
Word Hot
The Poet's Zodiac
The Countess of Flatbroke

Anthologies
The Lillian Trilogy
Lavender Review
Lady of the Moon
Irresistible Sonnets

Children's Book
Nuts in Nutland

The Lillian Trilogy

MARY MERIAM

The Lillian Trilogy

MARY MERIAM

Word Hot

Conjuring My Leafy Muse

Girlie Calendar

HEADMISTRESS PRESS

Word Hot © 2013 by Mary Meriam.
Conjuring My Leafy Muse © 2013 by Mary Meriam.
Girlie Calendar © 2014 by Mary Meriam.
The Lillian Trilogy © 2015 by Mary Meriam.
All rights reserved.

ISBN-13: 978-0692377062
ISBN-10: 0692377069

This book may not be reproduced, in whole or in part, including illustrations, in any form (beyond that permitted by Sections 107 and 108 of the U.S. Copyright Law and except by reviewers for the public press), without written permission from the publishers.

Cover art by Florine Stettheimer "A Model (Nude Self-Portrait)" ca. 1915, oil on canvas. Used with permission of the Avery Architectural & Fine Arts Library at Columbia University.

Cover & book design by Mary Meriam.

PUBLISHER
Headmistress Press
60 Shipview Lane
Sequim, WA 98382
Telephone: 917-428-8312
Email: headmistresspress@gmail.com
Website: headmistresspress.blogspot.com

For Lillian

CONTENTS

Book One
Word Hot

Who leaves me rootless	1
Lesbian Studies	2
Mountain Town	3
To Lillian	4
Portrait of a Woman Revealing Her Breasts	5
Avifauna	6
Personal Ad	7
Wedding Song for Two Women	8
Eau Sauvage	9
Cave In	10
The Woman of My Dreams	11
Night	12
An Entering	13
Melon Balls	14
Country Music	15
Port of Call	16
Thought in a Heatwave	17
Thoughts	18
So Close	19
iMuse iMoan	20
Anticipation's sweet	21
Muse of To	22

Book Two
Conjuring My Leafy Muse

1. Clink the iron
The Art of Ashes	27
Plaintive Note Motel	28
Wolf	29
Garden State After the War	30
Beginning with a Line from *Paradise Lost*	31
A Tragedy of Flowers	32
The Mother's Buttons	34
I Learn Today My Mother Lied	35

2. The heartbeat drums
How Beautiful She Is	39
Scene	40
Witness This	41
Orphic Chant	42
Madhouse	43
The Stone Insanity	44
Out of Time	48

3. Broken bell
Cuckoo Father	51
Sorry Show	52
Why won't you love me?	56

4. A hum, a hum, a hum
Crumb By Crumb	59
Lost	60
Animal Pity	61
The Only Home I Know	62
Midnight Kitchen	63

5. Drums at dusk

Night of Snow	67
Sweet Woman	68
Charlotte Mew	69
Sea de Sade	70
Somewhere Along the Spectrum	71
Three Crowns of Misfortune	72

6. Shrieking creatures

The Prince of Glass	77
Obodowka Cemetery	78
Arondeus	79
Dinner	80
Pine Needles on Snow	81

7. Burn and hum

Baptist Faggot Dinosaur	85
I'll Call Him Art	86
The Ozarks in 2004	87
The Sum of Fall	88
Done	90

8. Thundering swallows

Conjuring My Leafy Muse	93
Elegy for Charlotte Mew	100
Singular Heart	101
Epic	102
Cannot control the thunder	103
Hieroglyphics	104
You pierce me	105
The Acrobats	106
Muse of O	107

Book 3
Girlie Calendar

January
Wu Tsao's Seclusion	112
Sappho in Exile	115
The Lake	116
Bee Bouts-rimés	117
Beginning with a Line by Robert Frost	118
The Loser	119
Stationmaster	120

February
The Boston Soak	122
Valentine	123
To Elizabeth Bishop	124

March
Soup	126
Farewell to my delight	127
On the 40th Anniversary of Lillian & Phyllis	128

April
Prayer for Leaf	130
Trip Triolet Trio	131
My Rhona	132
Facts About Romance	133
Comfort Song	134
Elaine	135
I wanted you	136

May
Birdhouse	138
Hot Spell	139
What We Do	140
Red Kiss	141
Had We But	142

June
Ladies in Waiting	144
What rhymes with breasts?	145
may the women in prison dance	146
Girlhood	147
How Like You This	148
A Garland of Sighs	149
Sonneglige	150
Gaze	151
World	152

July
The Romance of Middle Age	154
Lingua Lesbian	155
Eureka Springs	156
Dance of a Dozen Lovers	157
Workshop Romance	158
Farmer's Market	159
I'm still here	160

August
Seashore	162
Who's this coming out of the sun?	163
Vincent Van Go-Gogh	164
To Be Recited By Sappho On The Fourth Plinth In Trafalgar Square	165
And	166
When I Meet Her By the Seashore	167
On the Breakwater	168

September
The Great God Pollen	170
What will I do?	171
Daylight Losing Time	172

Lone Poem   173
Daylilies   174
Open Sea   176
Beginning to Dance   177
Futile the winds   178

October
Lighthouse Keeper   180
Anchor Hitch   181
Time   182

November
The Loser's Lament   184
Intersection   185
Enough   186
The Need for Reading   187
Sonett   188

December
A Cappella   190
You   191

Notes   192
Acknowledgments   194

Word Hot

Who leaves me rootless

You! all rich now? man at your cozy table,
tête-à-tête, now gets every murmur, whisper,
laugh and sigh that dreamily leaves your lips? How
sweetly your echo

slays my heart, my hard-ridden heart, that beating
harder, horse-whipped, stifles my voice. Now wordless,
bee-stung, broke, deserted, I look at you and
totally lose it.

Fire snakes and slithers, now blisters blazing
skin, now eyes lose eyesight, now eardrums beat drums,
sweating rain, now race in a thunder tremble
whirlwind tornado

green as grass I'm taken, a prisoner chained in
ravaged daisies. Where is my mind, my flower—
petal-plucked and rootless. Be brave now Mary,
dirt poor but healthy.

Lesbian Studies

O my muse, promiscuous muse, my bunny,
hop off paper, hop in my arms, my darling
muse not mine, my everyone muse, please let me
touch and amuse you.

Now the past is sliding away, past harm's way,
past the nightmare hidden in sex's dream, when
you, in need, decided to strip and show your
body to die for.

Naked, word hot, here are your breasts, *I'm breathless
writing this, yes throbbing and flushed,* your memoir's
pictures move me far from a text perusal,
write me, I'm lovesick.

Mountain Town

Dear morning moon above
                              the crumbling stairs
a precious book
                    a landing where I raise
my eyes to see you,
                         make me understand
the steps to take to you
                              here in the trees
the tiny castle built
                         of old gray stone
the stairs so steep and cracked
                                   the day so young
the doors still locked   I wait
                              I breathe
                                        I find
the shadow of the biggest tree
                              for shade.

Another trip,
                         across the morning sky
a jet drags two thin streams
                              of ghostly cloud
a path I think you take
                         so far above me.

Inevitable flower blooms
                         alone
naked, pink, and tall:
                         one Naked Lady.
I read and borrow
                    borrow, read
                                        return.

To Lillian

Some summer nights, it seems like you are mine,
a lilly dream grown out of loneliness,
when all my sepals, stems, and petals pine,
and I can almost hear you saying yes.
But no, your flower bed is closely tended.
There's nothing you can do with my bouquet.
The past and all its sorrows have been mended;
likewise, my lilly dream should fade away.
Should fade away as summer flowers fade,
petal by petal falling to the ground,
singing a sad and lonely serenade,
wilted and dizzy, lost and strewn around.
It seems the lilly dream is mine to keep,
pressed tight inside these pages, fast asleep.

Portrait of a Woman Revealing Her Breasts

Sensing Tintoretto's brushes
on her breasts, tender, luscious,
she looks away and faintly blushes.

Can we understand the deal
she made to model and reveal?
Was it for love? Oh, let me feel

this love, then let my fingers slide
along each folded, flowing side
of parted dress and salty tide,

until I touch her strands of pearls.
Now tickled by her auburn curls
and wavy locks, her image twirls

an ocean where I cannot swim
and flailing, drown. Here on the slim
shore of sound, I sigh and limn.

Avifauna

Somewhere in the world tonight,
    someone waits for me;
her red silk slippers of delight,
    her blue room by the sea,

her tangerines, her house of words,
    her tragedy and play,
seem close as all these singing birds,
    and likewise, far away.

Personal Ad

Lap me
         languish me
                  lake my longing
Here on earth
     no gunshots, no hunger.

Dreamworld of eyelids relaxing
Earlobes receptive to sound

You across the table, looking at me
You in the hammock, the bath, the bed

Walking the fields on the swallowtail path,
Wounded but alive, pulsing with courage.

Let me touch her. Let her be you.

Wedding Song for Two Women

Didn't I always know this leaf
in some cathedral in my mind
impossibly high with green relief
was with me intertwined?

Wasn't it her inside my book,
the queen of chance and understanding,
and wasn't she why I undertook
my painted look at landing?

Oh, falling this way, the light, the air,
this feeling through the atmosphere,
this holding her hand and kissing her there,
without her being near

the saddest edge of the spinning world,
this knowing and never knowing before
the stems and vines of longing curled
around her open door.

Eau Sauvage

Two windows weeping lilac curtains, sheer
and long, and lilac bushes perfume air
from snowy peaks. A quiet room, austere.
A mattress on the floor, a desk and chair.

The disco dancers throbbing in the dark,
drinking and drunk. Speed shots of burning light.
I go there. Why then does this woman park
herself in front of me and break the night?

Her eau sauvage for men. Her downcast eyes.
Her short black hair. *Intoxicate my mind,*
Professor. Say your body tells no lies.
Loosen your full white bosom from its bind.

At last seduced, I kiss her on the lips.
Again, again, the driving downbeat whips.

Cave In

The forest sighs for succulent romance.
The moonlight jiggles in a modern dance.
The waiting window holds the weary tree.
The midnight branches tap. Come back to me.
My bed of fallen needles scares the crow.
My frost left all the crickets in distress.
My earth is certain nothing green can grow.
The threads get weaker in my careless dress,
and I have lost the will and way to sew.

The Woman of My Dreams

At last, the hour strikes to go to sleep.
She waits for me—there's no one else. Her face,
at first, reflects the moon, then her embrace
embroiders cloaks to hide the very deep.

As I begin to fall to sleep, I reap
the whole day's dreams. My sleep is wearing lace.
She lullabies me to a calmer place,
then fastens me with pearls and lets me weep.

Night

Darling night, again I address your distance,
cricket racket, owl on the prowl, the letter
Z in bubbles, blankets and sheets, your pillow
        making me heavy,

oh, the wait for you to undo your buttons,
let your swiftness go through the open window,
moonward while the weight of you stays, unfolds, and
        blooms with an orchid's

sweet-sick scent; but when you descend on me, good-
night, the distant fire arrives and takes me
down with you, much deeper than sense, to private
        radiant oceans.

An Entering

I am asleep on my city's dead street,
when you take my hand, and then we are walking;
there is silence, but I can feel your hand talking,
pulling me deeper into your warm, sweet
language, speaking to me, with a teacher's eloquence,
of your need, which is beginning to dawn on me
in the dark theater, where no one can see
the tutorial of your kisses, which are kindling the sense
of warmer and closer things yet to be known—
how could I then awaken, hideous, alone?

Melon Balls

What do I know of sex in my seclusion,
the big black bull outside the hot barbed wire,
the female rancher's sweat in the confusion,
for all I know, the bad bull's balls on fire?
I'm most familiar with my quiet table,
with casseroles, with roasted nuts and seeds,
with stewing beans, with salads cool and stable,
with satisfying simple daily needs.
A smooth-skinned melon? Yes, it fits my hands.
I feel the melon's soft warm weight and think
of her. A lizard nods. He understands?
I rinse the melon in the kitchen sink
and try to let my thoughts run down the drain.
The absence of her pleasure is my pain.

Country Music

It was because I dreamed of you again,
and soggy leaves were sticking to my shoes,
and I was tired of listening to men,
that you again seemed closer than a muse.
I went outside to catch a breath of air,
the wind blew in my face like a surprise,
warmer for fall, it seemed, than it was fair,
but colder air was lurking in disguise.
And all around my mind, the monstrous dome
of heaven clings to hell beneath my feet,
choosing which way I walk away from home,
kicking the leaves, as if my incomplete
existence could be saved without you near,
as if a wish could make a muse appear.

Port of Call

Nothing but touch will ever satisfy
my storming surge of lust for you.
         Appear
  dikes moan.

      Come near
waves lash.
        Come close

         gulls cry.

My burning vessel flaunts the flag sincere.

Way to the west, my rusty bark is sighted,
though lately stuck in piddling inland lakes.
Her signal flares

  Condition Unrequited

yet see the spray her bonny bow shape makes.

My wish runs whistling through the dusky air,
laden with galley-cook and sailor cries,
to gaze at the blue, blue sky of your sultry eyes,
and sniff your wavy, salty spring of hair,
to find the smooth pink shell of your perfect ear
and breathe
    it's you
      it's you I want
come here.

Thought in a Heat Wave

The words, the books, the strain,
the loneliness, the pain,
the beast of woe, the lion roar,
it doesn't matter anymore

because I have a thought,
tamed, soothed, caught:
the poetry I said to you,
the lines that led to you,

the arteries around my heart,
the words I read to you,
the breath and rhymes, the breathing in,
the us not dead to you,

the dancing of you in my dreams;
I could be wed to you;
my loveline veering off my palm
could go, instead, to you;

your jewel burning in my mind,
your brilliant cry, so kind,
your evening sky of cobalt blue,
yes, I think of you

and I together in one place,
with time and room to sigh,
and moved by magic to embrace
the body, you and I.

Thoughts

Some thoughts are too unbearable to think,
but still they rock me nightly, tidal waves
of worry, thoughts that knock me off the brink,
drown me, and bury me in shapeless caves.
Some thoughts are faces I once knew, and some
remember voices, visions, trouble, thunder,
and some thoughts dwell on what I have become,
and others flutter from the world with wonder.

I keep one thought apart from all the rest,
safe in a locket on a silver chain
around my neck, close to my pulsing breast,
my one thought safe from salty spray and rain
that soak my aspirations through and through.
Drown me again. My thought holds on to you.

So Close

O did I not? Yes soe did I
Mary Sidney

The owl so close, I see her fine
feathers of gold. She doesn't seem
to mind the snow. I see snow shine
like glitter on her coat, and dream
of you at my front door tonight,
like magic through the foot of snow,
or did you glide here and alight?
You step inside, we say hello,
then kissing you, I slide to the floor,
and every inch of you, adore.

But thou wilt not, nor he will not
Shakespeare

But now you have no time for me?
But who was I for all this time?
But is there someone I could be
so you would stay by me? Or I'm
not good enough, nor quick to change?
Tighter and tighter gets the knot
that binds you to this interchange?
You feel you've given all you've got?
But I grow roses in the snow
for you, so please, oh please don't go.

iMuse iMoan

please take me with you when you go
there's no one else i've asked this of
my darling muse i miss you so
please take me with you when you go
as light as air as still as love
a tiny pocket message glow

Anticipation's sweet

Anticipation's sweet, so shall we go there?
Here is my proposition apropos there.

You witness this, the book of my seclusion,
rollicking from my tongue, the words aglow there.

I watch your contrails through my windowpane,
the curtain parted for the distant show there.

And in this deep disturbance of my sleep,
a figure much like yours is dancing slow there.

Thicker and thicker honeysuckle vines,
sweeter and sweeter blossoms seem to grow there.

I make my little plans for future kisses—
there I begin, and there, until I know there.

The roundness of your chin, quite merciless.
Faint humming of a bee beneath the snow there.

Muse of To

To go somewhere, to drive a car, to fly,
to take a train or bus, go north or south,
or east or west, to hear your sounds, to cry
at words like music spilling from your mouth,
this fantasy, so simple, I could dream
through Russian tundra, down the city street,
through farmers' fields, across the frozen stream,
past fallen trees, away from my retreat.
To climb, to slip, to fall, to walk, to run,
to use my legs and feet to leap divides,
to ride the freeways, cloverleafs, the one
deserted road, until the daylight slides
to night, and like the pillow for your head,
to bring you all the words that should be said.

Conjuring My Leafy Muse

1. Clink the iron

The Art of Ashes

On the stones, the cinders linger,
Clink the iron, stink the stones.
Trace a pattern with my finger,
Stay away from rosy zones.

Can I make a fairy flower?
Can I draw her close to me?
Fairy, goddess, helper, mother,
Witch inside the flaming tree,

Bring your goodness to my ashes,
Bring a gold and silver gown
Bound with lace and silky sashes,
To the soot where I lie down.

In my dreams, the sound of swishes,
Like the broom that sweeps the stoop,
Fetches all my midnight wishes:
On an upswing down you swoop.

You are sweet, quick-witted, tender,
I am weepy by the wood
Blinded by the sight of splendor.
Wish I could.. I wish I could..

Plaintive Note Motel

Mother, are you lonely? I hear you sigh, then
moan in steady beats while you sleep beside me,
wounded moans, some tragedy never told me
    strangling your song-pipe.

Breath by breath, the moaning of Mother reddens,
death by drugs, flushed fugue, how she suffers sigh-sick
groans, while I, as always her daughter-stranger,
    ride my red wagons,

twist and trickle down on my twin slim bed in
Plaintive Note Motel, where we stay to witness
Kenny's wedding. Marriage, was that the trouble?
    Moaning, my mother's

stone unturned; a shot in the dark, my guesses.
Burned is Mother's everyday state, her fury
blackness brushes by on my rising nowhere,
    faster and faster.

Wolf

Mother, a wolf is wolfing me
Down. I thought I had a mother
But now I'm being wolfed. See?
Mother, a wolf is wolfing me
Down, your baby one sweet pea
Bit by hot teeth. I want another
Mother. A wolf is wolfing me
Down. I thought I had a mother.

Garden State After the War

O mommy, mommy, watermelon red,
my life is like a watermelon seed
you spit. Each night you tuck me into bed,
I need a spider swatted, or I need
the fruity sweetness of a juicy slice,
or whatsoever things are pure and true.
A bedtime story would be very nice,
your hidden past, the fact you are a Jew.
The watermelon's heavy in the bag,
and whatsoever things are good and just
are heavy too. O sweet and bitter drag,
the red, red flesh and rind of mother trust.
You are afraid, and so am I afraid.
Goodnight again, goodnight, my masquerade.

Beginning with a Line from *Paradise Lost*

Dreaming by night under the open sky,
waiting for heaven, I have no mother.
No, not this black-haired alien,
blood-red lipstick in the mirror.

The museum of modern art corridors,
the hallways of grade school echoing,
the stench of buses and lunchrooms,
everywhere I am, she is distant.

This is why my homework is homeless.
Only my checkered blankets love me.
Comfort me, my little pillow and bed,
dreaming by night under the open sky.

A Tragedy of Flowers

She says she is my mother, I'm her daughter.
I take a photo of her by the water,
blueberry picking, and her smile flowers.
But she abandons me in darker hours,
and so I search in the surrounding fields
for any mother-love the landscape yields.

There is a farmer with his summer yields.
I visit him as if I were his daughter
then nestle in the hollows of his fields
beside a tiny trickling stream of water,
and I weep there long and hard for hours,
twisting chains and whistles out of flowers.

There is a garden of my mother's flowers.
I wonder if the fragrances it yields
will tranquilize my mind for all the hours
I have left to be my mother's daughter;
or should I cross the muddy river water
or turn around and traipse the same old fields.

A herd of deer is bounding through the fields,
fleeing afraid, although I offered flowers.
They vanish in a hurricane of water,
and nothing in the sad sky-weeping yields
to prayers and wishes from a boggy daughter.
How much longer, harder, are the hours.

A storm's been threatening in the east for hours
and now I see it move across the fields.
It slashes lightning near the house's daughter,
my porthole's thunderstorm advances, flowers,
retreats, the way my mother never yields
a drop from all her barrels full of water.

My mother's flowers drink her howling water.
She caters to the flowers' needs for hours.
The creeper weaves, the blossom bends and yields,
and all around my mother's garden, fields
the farmer plows bow neatly to her flowers.
I wonder if she notices her daughter,

or if her daughter is a boat of water
sinking for hours or a clutch of flowers
strewing the fields until the tempest yields.

The Mother's Buttons

The mother sews with twitching round her eyes.
The daughter's wrist is bleeding in red streams.
The mother cries, and so the daughter cries.
The mother mutes the daughter's twisting screams
between her stricken breasts. The doctor stitches.
The daughter's smothered but all stitched together.
The mother knits. The mother's eyelid twitches,
and then the mother tugs the daughter's tether
tighter and tighter. And now the two at dusk
cannot forget the farmer's fragrant fields,
nor corn for dinner, shed of every husk
and boiled down. The silky twilight yields,
and goblins split the daughter's tousled head.
The daughter slides into the mother's bed.

I Learn Today My Mother Lied

"Not one drop of Jewish blood
in me or you!" my mother cried,
as if she had a drop to hide,
as if a drop becomes a flood
that drowns her in uncivil mud.
I learn today my mother lied.
"Not one drop of Jewish blood
in me or you!" my mother cried
and curtsied to the wigged M'Lud
until her Jewish spirit died.
Let my blood come back inside.
I drop her lying with a thud,
but not one drop of Jewish blood.

2. The heartbeat drums

How Beautiful She Is

She climbs the flights of palace stairs
Her gold and silver gown a charm
Whispering gone all troubles and cares
Worries and woes that cause alarm.

Tickled by rushing mountain streams
The gentle mountains kiss the sky
The sky alive with clouds and dreams
Sinking to dusk with one last sigh.

The fiddle sings, the heartbeat drums
While through the swirling, twirling court
The kindly prince of kingdom comes
As if a sailing ship to port.

Two turtledoves flush from a tree
As prince and maiden hand in hand
Begin to dance, this dance to be
A realm of peace, a fruitful land.

Scene

On the flowered couch in the dark, I see my
sister (blurred in memory) moving, sighing.
I'm a little innocent spy. A boy is
on her, excited.

Sisters doing dishes. The little sister's
weeping. Why? That boy, he was on you (taking
you so far from me). And the girl and faucet
weep in the kitchen.

Then comes clean the vase of this love for you, you
make me laugh, the night disappears, you splash your
little sister, yours, with your soft sweet flowers
flowing with solace.

Witness This

Hey little girl, come by, come by, and look.
It's time to watch your lovely sister die.
He says he wants to help, but it's a lie.
He'll steal her lovely life, by crook or hook.
He's in the kitchen, acting like a cook.
He's baking dreadful bread and poison pie.
Hey little girl, come by, come by, and look.
It's time to watch your lovely sister die.
She's sitting down. You see the bite she took?
Your tears mean nothing. Go ahead and cry.
Cry big fat baby tears and wave bye-bye.
She swallowed every morsel. How she shook!
Hey little girl, come by, come by, and look.

Orphic Chant

Let singer seek the way to hell,
and bring her back, and bring her back.
Let singer sound the hole of black,
and make her well, and make her well.
Let singer charm the deadly dell,
for knick the singer has a knack.
Let singer seek the way to hell,
and bring her back, and bring her back.
Let singer strike the silver bell.
Let singer ride the railroad track.
Let singer face the devil pack.
Let singer seek the way to hell,
and bring her back, and bring her back.

Madhouse

I'm sorry I'm too weak to break the walls.
I tried, I couldn't even shake the walls.
They call you crazy but you're only lost
sad sweet again my fingers rake the walls.
I drive to you two decades late. Forgive
my cowardice, I couldn't take the walls.
Here's where you sleep, the corner of a room.
Where is a room outside the ache the walls?
Your eyes are saying cigarettes and coffee,
the smoke the drink the pills the snake the walls.
We walk around the grounds of mental hell.
I pray for help for God earthquake the walls.
You say, *don't give the patients gifts, they'll never
stop demanding more, they flake the walls.*
A truck of groundsmen speeds by laughing leering
like you're prey for them. Mistake the walls.
I'm stupid sorry late, I'm dumb and scared,
but let me try. You must forsake the walls.
What nightmare leaves us broken as we kiss
goodbye. I'll tear them down the fake the walls.

The Stone Insanity

There's nothing I can do to change the past,
but still I am your mother, you my daughter.
I love you, and I'll show it now at last.
We sit on picnic benches near the water,
my heart in fragments on the grass. And then,
Sally's forgiven me; we're doing fine.
I know how much I hurt you two. Again,
my heart and soul slide helpless down my spine,
my hands can't catch the flowing from my eyes.
I'm sorry, please forgive me. Let me try.
To say the least, my acts have been unwise,
and all my life, I've handed you a lie.
These sweet maternal words, a wishing stream
rushing inside my mind, a mother-dream.

Rushing inside my mind, a mother-dream,
where every lie splits open, and true seeds
reach to the sun (while every dirty scheme
rots in the mulching pile with bitter weeds).
Where are my flower gifts of words for her?
I guess the world conspires to pull us low,
too many forces you could not deter,
some long-ago you never let me know.
(No pity for your daughters, heart of stone,
who tucked her babies deeply underground,
banished to stones, frozen in ice, alone,
an evil spell of exile, not one sound.)
My flowers blow away as fast as birds;
forgiveness isn't in my heart or words.

Forgiveness isn't in my heart or words,
but can I hope some supernatural hand
will send that flock of disappearing birds
back with a flower? Long enough to stand
a conversation woven in a crown?
Now listen up, my nightmare mother dear,
I'm still alive, you couldn't take me down.
Wake up, my mother-dream, my souvenir
of summer camps, piano lessons, food.
I will remember how you fed us well,
lucky for us, your rangy hungry brood,
your cats and puppies strewn around in hell.
I'm sorry for your pain, and sorry too
that there was nothing I could do for you.

That there was nothing I could do for you,
that I was nothing special in your life,
that you could simmer me for supper stew,
then calmly cut me with your fork and knife,
was swelter pain and milky wretch, was there
the house of changing hues, a ring of moods
and misery, the house of ill-repair,
each chamber with its own display of feuds,
the unraised waif discarded in a ditch,
another waif of love lost on the road,
and were you, mother, were you mother-witch?
and did you wart me like a daughter-toad,
and did you keep us parted and alone,
so that your secrets would remain unknown?

So that your secrets would remain unknown,
we lived like boarders in a troubled, hollow
silence, your phony sweetness on the phone,
the raging madness we were made to follow.
I stumbled through the fields and forests, dead
deer bones were everywhere, my tongue was torn.
Needier's land? kept pounding in my head,
and who owns this? and why I am forlorn?
I didn't understand you didn't care
if I was lost or hurt or murdered by
a beast. A child has nothing to compare.
It seemed your preference was that I should die.
As if to prove your fearsome witch's bite,
old Phillips' barn in flames inside the night.

Old Phillips' barn in flames inside the night…
We watched it from my room, as I recall,
across the fields, square in our line of sight.
It was a moonless summer night, with all
the fireflies ablaze, then Phillips' fire.
It could have just as easily been us,
but I made sure that no one would inquire,
and I would lie, and I would not discuss,
and I would hide myself forever from
the prying eyes of everyone, distract
and charm the world, until I would become
a member of society. It cracked,
this plan, directly on your daughters' heads.
Night watchmen drag us screaming from our beds.

Night watchmen drag us screaming from our beds,
while you knit sweaters in the living room
in pretty patterns, yellows, blues, and reds,
and in your garden, pretty flowers bloom.
Your ladies circle will be lunching soon,
your table is adorned with lovely plates,
a hum escapes, a merry little tune,
you sniff the hearty chowder that awaits.
Perhaps a speck of dirt is in your eye;
you never see your daughters' nightgowns flutter
in tatters down the stairs, goodbye, goodbye;
but just before we're gone, I hear you mutter,
(although the watchmen carry us so fast)
There's nothing I can do to change the past.

Out of Time

The moon, with all her starry sisters near,
moves slowly through the dark above my bed,
her clockwork ticking time off year by year,
observing both the living and the dead;
and when my tragedy of dreams is done,
all longings fully spoken for and counted,
a stronger light appears—it is the sun;
the horses of his regiment are mounted.

But once, I saw my sister in my sleep.
She held some dog-eared papers in her hand.
I wrote this novel. Take it. But the leap
of night to day will never understand
or stop for us, and she is gone again,
taking her words, her life, her book, her pen.

# 3. Broken bell

Cuckoo Father

Cuckoo father, hold my hand,
Come back from your cuckoo land.

Father never knew his heart,
I can't imagine how he could.
The surgeons measured every part,
And all they found was cuckoo wood.

Cuckoo father, flown away,
Come back cuckoo bird and stay.

The surgeons never made it well,
Father's heart was only sicker.
Keeping time no one could tell,
A wind-up clock, a cuckoo's ticker.

Cuckoo father, in the ground,
Come back with your heart unwound.

Sorry Show

I wish I could see him standing in the doorway of the living room.
He would have to be living. He would

have to be dancing to Big Bands on the stereo, making us
laugh because he was a grown man having a good time.

He would have to be a married man of the twentieth century,
with his mute trumpet corroding in the attic.

He kept his father's ashes on a shelf close by
his reading chair, and there an old green folder

holding my oldest poems, growing older,
and here is where nostalgia stops. Goodbye,

I could have said, my father could have said,
except goodbye requires a hello

and we were short of words.
I took his hand to cradle my heavy head,

to feel some comfort at the dinner table.
He gave me sugar-dusted toast with jam

so long ago, but was he kind? I am
his daughter from a past unstable

and burnt, with nowhere else to turn,
and for my father, of no concern.

I wish I could see her standing in the doorway of the living room.
She would have to be living. There would

have to be a doorway. Someone would have to be speaking,
or if not, listening.

World war two invades her mind again.
There is a sister left behind again.

If I could only see her one more time…
The memories begin to grind again.

Wisteria surrounds the patio
where dinner dramas will unwind again.

Which family dead steals pieces off the plate?
What solace will she ever find again?

You wretched tyrant eating like a pig—
I feel the wrench of mother bind again.

Turning me over to the muddy earth,
soaking me, and being unkind again.

I didn't know there was a war involved,
unwritten letters, love unsigned again.

The kitten eaten by the German shepherd—
be blind and deaf, and deaf and blind again.

The tissue house would have to be absorbing the hurricane
rains, and I would have to be riding my bike

up a hill so long it would have to be a mountain, or I would
have to be taking speed on the university campus.

Shot down by sorrow and weeping in the heavy brush
of scarlet-berried briers, bloodied, sounds of boots,

this the poison of the mother-witch's lexicon,
and I, a slight raw girl, stone-tongued and trod upon,

until my growing arms and legs grew into roots,
watered by my own eyes in my tortured hush.

How green the grass would have to be on the lawn around
the living room,

and how poignant the folk song
on the record player.

Why did I live? my whole life passed without you,
my helpless hands to save you, vast without you.

I've long since lost the golden chain you gave me.
The world you made for me fell fast without you.

Some say I'm not all here, or anywhere—
I can't explain the icy blast without you.

If you can hear me through the wall, don't answer—
this half a pearly shell must last without you.

Someday *la mer* may bring us back to shore.
Till then, my sorry show's miscast without you.

Why won't you love me?

Perhaps I am a broken bell,
a tumbleweed, an empty shell.
Perhaps I am a lonely child
by her loneliness beguiled,
under a witch's evil spell.

Perhaps I am an ocean swell,
a penny in a wishing well,
a piece of paper neatly filed.
Perhaps I am a broken bell,

a flower with a sour smell,
a secret locked in never tell,
a garden gone to seed and wild,
a statue toppled and reviled.
Farewell, farewell, farewell, farewell.
Perhaps I am a broken bell.

4. A hum, a hum, a hum

Crumb By Crumb

Inside the forest, I become
its sticks and twigs and silky thread
and leave my traces, crumb by crumb,

the trace of mummy, drowned in rum,
and daddy's dress in fed-up red.
Inside the forest, I become

them saying *scram,* and *do not come
back home again to your own bed.*
I leave my traces, crumb by crumb,

and ward off witches with a hum,
a hum, a hum, a hum, I said.
Inside the forest, I become

a mumbler asking, *are you dumb
to feed the birds your tasty bread,
to leave your traces, crumb by crumb?*

I wish to know where I come from,
but do not know, so walk ahead
inside the forest I become,
and leave my traces, crumb by crumb.

Lost

I ring the bell. The mademoiselle is lost?
I am, I answer, and my bell is lost.

I sell my cookies in the neighborhood,
but hopelessly, my clientele is lost.

Out on the gray-blue bouncing waves, my boat's
at sea, my fish is tossed, my shell is lost.

The menace multiplies on city streets
conquered by crows; my sad hotel is lost.

Where is my book of creatures? I could read
myself to sleep, but my gazelle is lost.

There is no love-god living on my road.
My riverbed is lost, my well is lost.

I marry no one, shadows in my eyes,
color myself, my last pastel is lost.

Animal Pity

What am I doing alone here in the park?
Caging me like a zebra in the zoo
would make me better cared for. Give me dark
to hide my horse-whipped flesh from public view.

Behind cold bars, a pair of lions screw.
In front, some jackass fools look on and mock.
A roar escapes, a roar that shakes me through.
Breaking through cage on cage, through lock on lock,

it hits Fifth Avenue, then leaps the block,
rips up the haute couture and banker's sack,
sends rippling thrills through Broadway's pigeon flock,
answers to no one, takes its grandeur back.

Now as the steel-blue evening stills the city,
I cuddle a small soft sound, a sound like pity.

The Only Home I Know

How do I know which railroad tracks to cross?
The bridge collapsed, the trail got washed away,
the highway signs went blank, the albatross
flies backwards, and I cannot find my way.
Oh world, oh world! forsythia in spring,
the cottontail in clover, leaves and snow
falling and falling over everything,
the years spin gold, go fast, go slow,
but where to go eludes me, as I drift
to bed, alone, undressed, prepared to sleep.
The crows are quiet; it's the cricket shift.
As usual, I close my eyes and weep,
my soft bed like a solitary boat
taking me somewhere, keeping me afloat.

Midnight Kitchen

You cross the river
on the bridge of your desire,
river ice, river wine, river fire
driving you to find her

practicing her cello
in her midnight kitchen,
one dim bulb yellow
in antique Pennsylvania.

You scratch the door,
your blood half wine.
She draws her bow
across your core.

No soloist, no orchestra,
has ever known
the score of silent sounds
you listen to alone.

5. Drums at dusk

Night of Snow

She lives, more lovely than sweet dreams,
Red berry lips, black hair that streams
In tender breezes through the night
Lit by starlight and pure snow white.

Meanwhile, her mother sits and schemes
Suffocating in her screams
At her own beauty's furious flight,
Old age's creeping, seeping blight.

She is the Queen, and her regime's
A bloody plot of swift extremes.
Her daughter's heart would taste just right.
She opens wide and takes a bite.

Through woods and thickets of thorny themes,
Snow stumbles through a night that teems
With lurking lowlife. Shot by fright,
She runs, and running, learns to fight.

Finally through the gloom there beams
The warm and friendly homelike gleams
Of seven gems. They are polite;
Snow's safe and snug at last? Not quite.

The lonely door has lost its seams,
Squeaks open for a witch who seems
Kindly, but murders with all her might,
To be the only belle in sight.

The tables turn again. Fate deems
The daughter live. The mother steams
In oven shoes, dancing her spite
To death, ever bitter and tight.

Sweet Woman

Did I ever know such a sweetness? Woman,
woman, when and where did I lose your scent? I
search and search my memory for those signals.
    Say I'll remember

soon, and kiss me, wake me, remind my body
lonely, touch is lovely and wanted dearly.
Woman, woman, there in the room, repairing
    close and together,

this, this thought can't conjure your hand or weight you,
ghost, blue witch, blue lack of a substance, vestige,
no, your eyes, and no, your fresh lips, and no, two
    there in the doorway.

Charlotte Mew

The she who writes of her is me.
The she who bites my lip is her.
One her, two she, and zero he.
The she who writes of her is me.
When she plus she is clearly we,
the she will show who we prefer.
The she who writes of her is me.
The she who bites my lip is her.

Sea de Sade

Marquise, dear darling bitch of decadence,
enough about your love for ancient Rome.
Let's reminisce about our close events.
You chased me, caught me, slayed me, brought me home,
proud master hunter in pursuit of prey.
Fainting I followed, wide-eyed, silent, high
on scotch and cigarettes. Quick came the day
you dumped me with a strangely sweet goodbye.
"Come here and sit," you said, "upon my lap."
"Oh, I'm too big," I moaned, "so tall, so big.
I can't." Was I so big? Well, no. Tap-tap,
you tapped, and so I sat, a sinking brig,
unmoored from the mother ship of culture, drunk
on masochism, and by a sadist sunk.

Somewhere Along the Spectrum

I take a class in feminine approach.
I hold my breath about my boyish clothes.
There is a subject I'm afraid to broach,
and for this fear I'm granted one red rose.
She smells so good, I wonder what she knows.
We leave the class together, go downtown
and dance. The beat goes fast and then it slows
until the slowness seeps inside and down.
Down to the dancing floor I fall and drown.
The dancers strip me clean of every shred
of gown and every penny in my crown.
I leave the Duchess, bleeding from the head,
naked and blind to nakedness, a mist
below the radar of the feminist.

Three Crowns of Misfortune

I. Stripper

Down the tawny, blood-red, and orange cast-offs
fall, like fairies tossing their crinkled clothing,
party-worn and faded in golden slants of
    earth-sinking sunlight;

all the Loves undone with her frock come falling,
dress undressed, unbuttoned, unzipped, Misfortune,
barefoot, rootless, stripped of her silver tree bark,
    shivers for strangers.

Not for strangers! Pitiless Love with velvet
gloves demands this stripping of leaf and costume,
downward dancing, falling forever, falling,
    falling forever.

II. Sweatshop

Wait for nothing, wait for the Loves, what matter
night that gallops, tramples her roses, horses,
wildmares, slung here fruitless and starved, Misfortune
    slips on the cliff's edge,

falls and falls with no one to catch her, over
rock face, street lamp, oceans apart from comfort,
mother, sister, lover; she sighs now, listen:
    love is unlikely.

Melancholic silkiness, cobalt, Loves hum
blue, the sidewalk saddens in Spanish Harlem
drums at dusk, at midnight, then morning traffic
    trumpets her shortfall.

III. Hack

Through the elms and ginkgos, alert to all her
listing, shrinking, deviance, sunk tomorrow,
no tomorrow ever, for sorrow's lonely
    arrows transfix her.

This is dark desertion, and silent, bitter
cold. She sits alone in the automobile,
waiting. Danger shoots her. The Loves go quickly
    somewhere without her.

Now the wheel is seized by some force outside her.
Death will drop her over the bridge. Misfortune,
desperate, poisoned, jinxed, a forgotten fire,
    fights like a soldier.

6. Shrieking creatures

The Prince of Glass

He is the prince of shards of glass,
glass bowls with Chinese stamps,
glass crystal balls with legs of brass,
and Tiffany glass lamps.

The prince has chosen to amass
glass window and glass door,
glass shelf and goblet, to surpass
his foes, who might have more.

So when he sees the lovely lass
in glass, he falls in love.
He plinks her coffin on the grass
with his glass-fingered glove.

He hates the forest's green morass
of trees and shrieking creatures;
with her in glass, they can't harass
her quintessential features.

The prince pulls out his looking glass
to check his golden locks.
The other things he does, alas,
are unseen from her box.

Obodowka Cemetery

This is dark, this time hell-sent,
This fending off the pack
That for your body tussles, bent
To sniff you and attack.

Already dogs have snapped away
Both your sister's feet.
Your naked little son is prey
They tore apart to eat.

Your body lies in sparkling frost
So new you seem to move.
My hands can only scrape a lost
Grave, a shallow groove!

Tomorrow, you and they must rot
Together in one pit.
I'd gladly go with you, and not
Wander off from it.

(after Alfred Kittner's "Friedhof Obodowka")

Arondeus

Is this why I was born,
to dress in rags and beg from friends?
Put here to paint, to write?

I met a man who labors to feed us,
barely fed. My Jan, remember
how naked moonlight filled our bed?

When the blackest dogs
broke loose, I heard an angel
tell me how to move,

to bomb our registry of papers,
blast our names and numbers;
the Nazis' fangs dissolved in vapors.

My last words before they shot me:
Laat het bekend worden dat homoseksuelen geen lafaards zijn!
Let it be known that homosexuals are not cowards!

Dinner

Tonight I set the dinner table for
the remnants of my phantom family.
Here is the marriage spent in fantasy,
here is my stillborn brother, here is war
that wiped out all my relatives and tore
my mother's mind to pieces, here is me,
here is a place beside me for big tree,
and here's my sister shot down with a roar.
We flipped and landed upside down in hell,
no parachutes, just higher, hotter flames
burning our places right down to our names.
The empty plates have nothing left to tell.
Here is a table, here a fork and knife,
here is the phantom of a better life.

Pine Needles on Snow

Let me go, my memories, sack my country,
set a fire to it, release my dying,
let my natal mind be at peace. I'm ready.
    Lose me forever.

Couldn't, didn't, wanted to save my village,
crawled the corridors underground, kept hoping
this was it. I thought this was earth, my planet,
    people who loved me.

Saving, raving mad, they are all collapsing
buildings, crouched on streets, unforgiving, desperate,
crazy. Let the savior defeat the witness,
    finish the story.

7. Burn and hum

Baptist Faggot Dinosaur

I'm at pump ten trying to sound rational in my mind. What is this gas, dinosaur bones? Then a siren, and since this is Arkansas, I hear a cop screaming faggots. Yes, I think gas comes from Earth, and that's where dinosaur bones are piled. They had to die somewhere, right? There must be tons of bones and dinosaur teeth. A van of baptists from Oklahoma stops at pump nine. They're from Earth too. I think Earth is made of dinosaurs, which were almost as big as Earth. One foot was like as big as Hawaii. They hopped around from Hawaii to Alaska to Manhattan. Continental drifts and divides meant nothing to them.

I'll Call Him Art

Art is undone. His chair's askew. His eyes,
his eyes are locked with mine. His look is raw,
mascara running, caught by small-town law,
the bible belt, bewildered parents' sighs.

Art is a man-child boy-girl compromise,
sitting between his farmer maw and paw,
here in the sheriff's office, Satan's claw.
Art holds the Word of God, holds back his cries.

I'm helpless, Art, to save you, where we are.
I try to say all this with one quick glance
before I go. Let's both go, shed the scar
of twisted stares. Let's cut and run. Let's dance.
You'll tell me all about it in the car.
Coyote-howl away the circumstance.

The Ozarks in 2004

On days like this, when no one knows or cares,
I'm sitting with her in connected chairs
that roll the thigh to touch the other's thigh,
this minor touch a dreamy contact high.
While most of me is focused on our mission,
I do consider this a good position.

She stands in front of me against a wall,
we stand together in a narrow hall,
perhaps she's climbing in her mountain mind.
I shift from foot to foot, and when I find
my voice, we talk a while about back East.
She's homesick. So am I, to say the least.

Police with guns stand guard against the crowd
gathered to hear her speech. I sit there proud
and frightened while her words burn and hum,
securing for us the auditorium.
She gives us courage, and we give her cheers,
but still this hateful place can kill us queers.

The Sum of Fall

Outside, surprised, you see a flare of red.
It is a fox, lit by the sun, I said.
The fox glides by. That is the sum of fall
for us, outdoors. Then you give Steve a call
about the trees to trim and dead tree wood
that he should cart away. *Is Thursday good?*

As good as fox can get, whose gliding's good,
whose tail in slanted sun turns fire-red.
*Please take the fifty-foot dead ash, for wood
to sell or burn as you see fit,* you said
to Steve. He'd check his week then give a call.
The red fox-tail, the walk we took this fall.

The ash is dead, and wind could make it fall
right on our house, with us inside. Not good
how long it took to give this guy a call.
I try to hold the image tight, fox-red
in slanted sun, the glide. Steve called and said
that Thursday still is looking good; he would

be here to chop the ash tree down for firewood.
I stand outside with Steve. *The ash will fall
safely, away from us, I'm safe,* he said,
this giant fireman. I see he's good
with ladders, ropes, and saws. He's used to red-
hot crises, used to falls, the desperate call,

but does Steve know we had no one to call
when they would burn our house like firewood?
They torched bonfires day and night, the red
flame flicking near our house, in spring and fall,
the devils tried to drive us out for good.
You don't belong with us, the sheriff said.

Get out, get lost, go back, the whole world said.
We stay inside; there's no one left to call
but Steve, who felled the dead tree, clean and good,
then sawed the trunk in chunks and took the wood
to sell or burn, as he sees fit. The fall
leaves turn, lit by the sun, turn gold and red,

but we were good, no matter what they said.
The wild geese call, we saw the red fox glide,
and creatures cry all through the wood in fall.

Done

Quarter to nine, the trouble in the sink is done.
The trouble from a day spent on the brink is done.

The walk we took at two, the two of us alone
in weather strangely warmer, in a blink is done.

The field of small white asters, bees and butterflies,
the buzz and scent of them, the pleasant stink is done.

It happens every fall, the leaves are green then gone,
scattered and run aground, poor leaf, its link is done.

Even with so much earthly danger, even so,
we're never done with love, or what we think is done.

I've felt her soothing over me, the sweetest spirit.
She is ineffable, so Mary's ink is done.

8. Thundering swallows

Conjuring My Leafy Muse

Dear lady of the lake,
don't leave me stranded here
with owls and mousey prey.
You take my ache away.
I need your hands to hold me,
not to tease.
I park my rusty car on leaves,
all layered, wet, and brown,
and see the sky, all pewter gray.
Down the slope,
the lake is higher,
not so far from where I stand.
I just can't read your eyes
that shine like spring Nebraska skies,
your pale Midwestern prairie eyes
that show no depth
and give no clues.
The earth accepts the sun.
The earth accepts the moon.
We live our days and nights
on earth apart.

Dear pot of boiling beans,
you boil over.
You dance away.
You care for nothing but the dance.
You sound a little sad.
Retracing steps I knew,
a narrow hall,
the dressing room,
I knock.
I knew the sea inspired you while you swam.
I felt the buzz you felt in Provincetown.
I miss the scene,
secluded like a nun.
You know the tricks of distance,
the games that words can play.
I'm in the sticks, with beans.
I like how you've got better things to do.
You're grounded.
I wonder if I sounded
contrite, controlled, confused,
or simply gone.

Dear treasure chest of trouble,
crows fly around my house.
The mob is after me, they mock and sneer.
Deep inside my quiet room, I hear
your heart beat slow.
Your hair is loose and shines like gems.
I sail away and live on waves of you,
my pale disheveled body
finding harbor here,
my love, my dear.
I pluck a rose with petals
soft and swollen, scented sweet,
a blood-red rose that titillates my nose,
a red so red, it radiates with heat.
I fear my wanting you,
and feeling wrong for you,
but our minds roam like mariners
around the world.
We contemplate our trips,
you blowing words
across my cheek.

Dear perfect yellow leaf,
spearmint soap slips
along my slope of arm.
A bubble forms. I stretch,
it stays and grows,
a rainbow-flecked thin skin of haze
that glistens, pops, goodbye.
I close my eyes and find I am alone
without my bubble.
This feels like
yet another kind of trouble.
We sit on benches near a brook.
You see the clouds on cue,
the drama passing east to west.
I'm scared of my own life,
my death was very close,
my slow return took centuries.
Unsure of what to do,
lying on a bed of grass,
unsure of being yellow in July,
a perfect yellow leaf considers fate.

Dear late green leaf,
already summer thinks of fall,
forgets the spring, the rush to green.
I am the leaf, the late green leaf,
the leaf that used to safely hang
among the other leaves.
I walk away.
It's long past due.
I won't be waiting, or hoping, or happy hearing,
or best wishing you.
I will no longer care how you are coping.
Forgotten touch, save me,
if you could just.
Never mind, I'll catch some other wave.
Unless you think another way,
a certain way,
oblivion without the decadence.
I might feel lost,
peruse the word and feel bereft,
perpetually homeless,
tied to it, the longing and the loss.

Dear troubled years,
I lie awake and gaze at dark.
The fan, a steady hum.
The moon.
Feeling fills the room and longs for you.
I'll send an envelope to you. Inside,
I'll put my house, my heart, poetic tears,
the crooked pages of my rainbow pride,
and fifty troubled years.
Then the night words scatter.
Then lost in work,
the words stay hidden.
As if to change the world,
my words could matter.
Syntax cut from cosmic lust.
I bang the keys.
I dance on air but never fly.
My drawings disappear inside a breeze.
Then pen and paper,
with words, I am,
and solitude becomes my diadem.

Dear end of time,
I drive lorn hills alone.
The miners are alive, then dead.
This is my work, my home,
my lover. You say that's fine,
your body's busy elsewhere
till the end of time.
My love, I cannot find the form
to name my sighs.
My theory dies.
My love, give me faith that I can rise
and say that this is such and such or so and so,
and yes,
that is correct, and this I know.
I feel your fingers touch my face,
but you're not there.
I feel the form will let me rest
forever in your arms.
I hope to hold and kiss you in the dark,
and so I turn
to burning words.

Elegy for Charlotte Mew

My heart drifts down, red-brown, a falling fall leaf.
Release, release, not knowing ground, a small leaf.

I dream you are beside me on a couch,
your blouse is white, I tremble, you are all leaf.

Do I not move the sun rootbound in summer
and fill your queenly crown with standing tall leaf?

Green of delight debarked despairing, lost.
Poem and letter flaming downfall, leaf.

Remember I gave you rings and poise and shimmer?
Who gave you shade is now a shadow thrall leaf.

My words were crimes were loves were leaves were smoke
Were gay were bashed were kiss were masked ball leaf.

You knew the seamstress never could repair us.
You knew November is my dance hall leaf.

With merriment no more, decay, embrace me,
at one with sky and dirt, a stone wall leaf.

Singular Heart

My heart hurts so. It slides like eels
in an aquarium.
Sucking its little cage, it feels
the slop of meriam

weighty and wildebeest, the squeeze
of skeleton and time.
It hums, a hive of bumblebees,
my honey, my sublime.

It aches for you. It is the road
you rambled on. It pines
and croaks and taps a secret code
for you, these very lines.

Epic

My love, when all my battles finally end
and down the cobbled hill I drive my car,
bumping on tired tires round the bend,
my body all one wound, my skin a scar;
and when bedraggled, I observe the star
rising like water to my thirsty eyes,
deep in the trembling darkness, still so far,
you wrap your arms around my world of sighs
and all my fallen angels fill the skies.

Most people have a family. I have flowers
but only in my mind. I have a view
of dying ash and oak, and sometimes showers
of snow or rain. The weather passes through
like everyone who comes and goes, but you.
You are the window of my best new year,
my faithful point of view, my lovely coo,
my apple crunch, my fresh warm bread, my cheer,
and in my wild poetic dreams, my dear.

I wake up empty, emptier than ever,
and naked cuddled close to my abyss
who strokes my nape and whispers *never, never,
will I accept the ruins of your kiss.*
Put on my crumbling clothes and reminisce
about the nothing day and nothing night
and say, it will be good, it will be bliss,
the soup is on the stove with all its might,
and though I have no language, I can write.

Cannot control the thunder

Are there no dancers on this solemn square?
Come come, she breathes, come violin my dreams.

Her penetrating Bach cantata beats
its blacksweet wings within my dreams.

Hallucinate her name her name her name
Mmm open open oh! Light! Pin my dreams!

Away nightmares! Unspook and spin my dreams.
You, you, my soothing pet, begin my dreams.

Hieroglyphics

Thunder's font is beautiful, dovelike, Sappho.
Thunder sings and clings to me, silence tells me
you are mist or water, and rain is scrawling
    runes on the water

where you are, so distant, your face in showers.
Jade, tornado green, then a slate gray changing
dull and gray, then fire and silver sparkles,
    silence, where are you?

waves reflect you, water is leaping higher,
tree by tree. They lean towards you, weaker branches
scorched by lightning, burnt by a gust of gorgeous
    thundering swallows.

You pierce me

You pierce me with a thousand styles of kindness.
Your lightning shocks the earth with miles of kindness.

While I'm asleep all night in my soft bed,
you pave my bedroom floor with tiles of kindness.

Like some mad queen insatiable for gold,
I hoard and count your priceless piles of kindness.

How could I help but loosen all my armor?
How could I not succumb to wiles of kindness?

The letter never sent, the gaze not met,
the words unsaid—all safe in files of kindness.

My terror at the thought of losing you,
as if I had you, oh! the trials of kindness.

What current took me out to sea, and now
turns me towards your murmuring isles of kindness?

You flood the sky of my unmarried dark,
you rise, a little moon with smiles of kindness.

The Acrobats

I spend my solo life in windy spaces,
way up above the throng, no safety net
below, exposed to row on row of faces
fixed on the acrobats in silhouette.
I'll fall with one misstep or if the wire
splits or my fingers slip. I climb the rungs,
trembling, trembling. Rising higher, higher,
I cough out all the fumbles in my lungs,
and here's my tiny platform, just a disk
that fits my feet. From here, I leap and swing
into the flashing lights, familiar with the risk
by now, but shocked to see you stand and fling
yourself from your own platform over there
and catch me from your swing through the thin air.

Muse of O

O lover, O my sweet sweet sweet sweet lover,
the O-ing letters of our alphabet
hide in the trees where wild blue tit birds hover
and make ah-sighs, their hearty beaks dew-wet,
their yellow-feather sides astir with fret.
You letter me, I letter you, we go
so high above the trees to do the pet
and bee, then with our O, we go below.
Down here, a hurricane begins to blow
and blow the leaves like Braille without a finger.
We tattoo dictionaries so we know
the tongue we speak, and let our language linger.
This is a sweet sweet sweet sweet afternoon,
the education of our lover rune.

Girlie Calendar

January

All January wanted was a home,
and not these crows, and not these frozen trees,
limbful of snow. It was a home, with these:
a door to close, a chest of drawers, a comb.

Wu Tsao's Seclusion

January 16
my toes touch the soft edge
of my new mattress
soft as the bare breast of a lover
soft as the rainfall tonight
patting and tapping the sodden ground

and the memory of her scent arousing
and blinding me lingers decades later
like a satsuma tangerine's
sweet-sour soaking of my mouth

February 1
chance of snow tonight
will we get out tomorrow
to pick up the mail?

February 7
it's Saturday night
I'm too busy having fun
no time for haikus

February 14
the supermarket check-out clerk's
warm ready smile
penetrates my sore mood,
fluorescent lights, my failures

"I remember you don't need receipts,"
she says, showing it, taking it back,
and laughing playfully

I smile and let my good wishes wash
all over her, her feet standing for hours,
and all the troubles found
in supermarket check-out jobs
for older married ladies

February 23
February ends
clouds gray
black cows and cow pies dot the fields
skunks and cats dead
roadside decoration
sixty miles I drive
a narrow path through farms and hills
three horses munch whatever's left
hawks, eagles, crows, vultures prey
my winter mind
wakes up in town today
when walking down the empty aisle
she approaches me
with eyes that speak my language
richly colored eyes that gaze directly
into mine and laugh
later, by chance, our eyes meet again
and sing and dance

March 29
ah, middle age,
I have arrived at your empty castle
the guards have taken me away

my face no longer fresh enough for spring
that hits my mind with wind and rain
and sweet delicate pastel little flowers
instant everywhere
your crime lives on unknown
you only know that one by one
the ones you love are gone
and she took herself away
so why should I care
I will not allow myself to ask
but I will remain silent
and listen to the chirping birds

Sappho in Exile

How would I know the city? By
a thousand cuts or one hello,
her dress of black or bad goodbye.

One sparrow from a tree would fly.
The traffic on the streets would flow.
How would I know the city? By

her look, the question in her eye,
her faith in false Pinocchio,
her dress of black or bad goodbye.

I love her still, don't ask me why.
Like others then, she had to go.
How would I know the city? By

the shock, the press, the loss of I,
the library, the picture show,
her dress of black or bad goodbye,

her hand reposing on her thigh,
her lion's paw of lasting woe.
How would I know the city? By
her dress of black, her bad goodbye.

The Lake

Suzanne, poetic fauna blues the lake,
forest full moon fish who cruise the lake.

What do I know in my van winkle world?
My old binoculars peruse the lake.

The past came back and hit me in the ass,
monstrosity who would abuse the lake.

The present drags me under every day.
The Osage homeless ghost tattoos the lake.

She was a poet and she killed herself.
What can I do about the bruise? The lake.

Promise to soothe the hurt and never hurt,
calling myself to task. The muse, the lake.

Unlock the throat, unlock the mind, and sing,
sing for the tongue-tied girls who lose the lake.

This merry lass an everblooming dreamer,
praying these ghazal waves transfuse the lake.

Bee Bouts-rimés

Today I wore my face called undepressed.
Tomorrow I'll put on my face of rain.
This switch of faces is a constant strain
but such is life, a queen bee's busy nest.
Some days I feel that God has knelt and blest
my bees, and other days God wraps a chain
around my wings that reaches to my brain.
When can I sleep, God, when can I rest?
Day after day I smell the stinky blast
of gardens wearing faces in a wilt.
God's coming back to save us any day.
Today I wander through the beehive built
of all the dregs I saved from my bee past,
my God face hidden in the eggs I lay.

Beginning with a Line by Robert Frost

They spoke to the fugitive in my heart as if it were leaf to leaf.
They spoke to me one windy day from the copse nearby my house.
Low in the night they rustled to thief and owl and addict and mouse.
Let me be deaf to the crash of trouble and the mighty underworld.
The pile of rotten branches and gold leaves lies there dead and swirled.
It would take every court in the countryside to count the fallen leaves.
The judges must number themselves among the dirt-thirsty thieves.
I live in a room of cold-toed winter glowing with no relief.
Wandering silent, muttered about, I move from grief to grief.

The Loser

I lost Aunt Peggy's silver ring.
I lost my sister's golden chain.
It seems like I lose everything.
I lost Aunt Peggy's silver ring.
If you should have a gift to bring,
be careful of my slippery drain:
I lost Aunt Peggy's silver ring;
I lost my sister's golden chain;
I lost the song I meant to sing.

Stationmaster

The clatter of the world goes by
and pulls along each passing day.
You search for light along the way
and long for someone standing by
to put the shame to every lie
and explicate the shades of gray
as, clattering, the world goes by
and pulls along each passing day.
You feel your every heartbeat sigh
with grief you cannot chase away
with friends who only can betray
with flowers that will always die,
as, clattering, the world goes by
and pulls along each passing day.

February

Make me the heart of February, please,
her sweet and frilly be-mine valentine,
shot through and through with love incarnadine
and holy scented essence of heart's ease.

The Boston Soak

She shovels the snow from her drive
then takes her Sunday bath.
What does she know that I don't know?
she wonders in her long soaking bath.
She does make me laugh.
How far would I have to drive?
She splashes and slides in her bath
forgetting what she knows or doesn't know.
Her own skin belongs to her
and hot bubbles, there is no drive,
it's only love, and love is like water
unencumbered by "he" or "she."
One last slosh of soaked loofah,
and she steps out of the bath.
Down the drain goes the water,
where it ends, she doesn't know.
Perhaps in the snow on her drive.

Valentine

I love you very much.
Come keep me company
Tonight in fantasy
Because we cannot touch.

This word you close your eyes.
This line my lips on yours.
This rhyme the heartbeat soars.
This stanza moans and sighs.

This verse is incomplete,
My images run dry,
Because the pronouns I
And you have yet to meet.

To Elizabeth Bishop

We were standing in the dim living room of a stranger
Night was upon us and you were to die the next year

You were small and your hand was small in my hand
Even if we had spoken, I only remember silence

We had both suffered in our separate lives
The pulse of your hand in my hand is alive

The suffering was immense in the room
We shared only silence and one touch

My lover was eager to introduce us
Yes, we were looking at each other

March

On windy nights in March, her stars align,
like satin stitches neatly placed in rows,
and for a moment, though the rough wind blows,
her needlepoint is part of the design.

Soup

spinach: I was sound asleep, so I guess the tornadoes passed me by
asparagus: snow flurries this morning, drove to bank anyway
garlic: banker forgot his notary stamp
shallots: drove banker to get his stamp
leeks: banker said mouse was running around the parking lot
corn: upset about the snow
carrots: no accumulation
celery: mailbox empty this morning
potatoes: both glad and sad
cabbage: washed dishes, watched moon rise
butter: wondered why moon had missing piece
bean stock: heard on radio moon eclipsed tonight
salt: forecast says 62 on Monday
pepper: thought you should know

Farewell to my delight

Yes, I could cling like honeysuckle vine,
except that half of love is letting go,
and doesn't pruning help the flowers grow,
and after all, I cannot call you mine.

Yes, like a baby, I could cry and whine,
except that childhood ended long ago,
and isn't comfort something I should know,
and after all, you've clearly drawn the line.

So I will say farewell to my delight,
the sun, the moon, the rain, the snow, the sky,
and all the plants and creatures of the earth,
and I will close the door and call this night,
and call myself a child who says goodbye
and sleeps away the grief for all she's worth.

On the 40th Anniversary of Lillian & Phyllis

If one could read the poem of a face,
then I've read yours and memorized the words.
Two lips for wit and bliss would be the case,
if one could read the poem of your face.
An honest ear, a tooth for truth, for grace,
two flirting eyes that flit like little birds.
If one could read the poem of a face,
then I've read yours and memorized the words.

April

When April weeps, the tears drip on her toes,
the water rises in the jade-stone lake,
a blue jay shakes the red-bud blooms awake,
in rainy light, the green grass rosy glows.

Prayer for Leaf

The last old leaves have blown away,
and I'm alone, undressed, and lost,
shivering in a new spring breeze
beside the lake that laps the shore.

Blossom me slowly, bloom me good,
and draw my fancy flowers nigh.
Maple me softly, oak me strong,
and let my close-green clothing grow.

Trip Triolet Trio

1.
I have to go pick up the mail,
and then make breakfast, lunch, and dinner,
then go to sleep, then without fail,
I have to go pick up the mail.
I won't have time to tell my tale.
At least I am a well-fed sinner.
Now I must go pick up the mail,
and then make breakfast, lunch, and dinner.

2.
Ah bella Maria, the barber is singing,
the barber is snipping, the barber is dancing,
the barber is trimming, the phone is ringing,
ah bella Maria, the barber is singing,
the barber is humming, the barber is flinging
steamed green beans, the barber's romancing,
ah bella Maria, the barber is singing,
the barber is snipping, the barber is dancing.

3.
I cross from Missouri to Arkansas
on Fridays to shop in town, tra la.
With turtles and vultures and crows, caw-caw,
I cross from Missouri to Arkansas.
The sound of these states is stuck in my craw.
I'm stuck in the states of blah and blah.
I cross from Missouri to Arkansas
on Fridays to shop in town, tra la.

My Rhona

Ah yes, I scrutinized *The Art of Meeting
Women,* and fell for Rhona Sacks, her eyes,
her friendly smile, her hand held out in greeting,
her quick chit-chat. My Rhona is so wise!
I'd like to ask her, "Hey, what happens if
I'm not afraid, I'm not a slob, I say
hello, I'm cheery, kind, and not too stiff,
but she just doesn't care?" "Well then, don't stay,"
my Rhona pithily advises, "Move."
Helpfully, my Rhona urges lots
of get up, go, and find another groove.
"And if I'm stuck in her hard-hearted plots?"
"Break free," my Rhona counsels, "and be true
to the Rhona that I introduced you to."

Facts About Romance

The neighbor's cat is here again.
A heron bombs the silver blooms.
Moonrise lights the soggy tombs.
I go to sleep, wake up, and then,
who can tell me why or when,
creeping by the witchy brooms,
the neighbor's cat is here again.
A heron bombs the silver blooms.
Swear and sign it with a pen!
Follow her, the verdict looms.
Rush her from the rising rooms,
the bed of lavender, the wren.
The neighbor's cat is here again.

Comfort Song

In the town
She heals with words,
She wears a gown
Of berry birds.

In the city
She flies around,
She dons a pretty
Breeze she found.

How I miss
Her leafy park
And tulip kiss
In my cold dark.

Elaine

Elaine! I loved your face, your hands, your voice,
your touch, your mouth, your teeth, your toss
of light sweet aching hair,
the winding way you came across
the river to my bed. Our small-town fame
grew long along the muddy Delaware,
then we were swept away, our slant affair
not strong enough to swim against the tide
but stuck in narrow straits and forced to hide,
till you, Elaine, left me alone,
unknown.

I wanted you

I wanted you. Instead, I got the moon.
Who wouldn't stop her rising? Not the moon.

Put collard greens in noodle casserole,
spring onions, chard, and stir the pot, the moon.

Rain, rain, refrigerator, shower, thunder,
blood summer patio—how hot the moon.

The little virgin forest, thickets, leaves,
a locket round the lake, my cot, the moon.

Who tugs her sacred through the sky, the night?
Who rings the bell, but who forgot the moon?

Like mares in May that thud the thorny ground,
I'm sleeveless in the lover plot, the moon.

May

The life they tell of May is a mistake.
They simply wanted her to love a man
she didn't. Skewed her voice to fit their plan.
Left May alone with her peculiar ache.

Birdhouse

Why do my bluebirds choose the spring to leave?
The greening grass insults my nest of loss.
The pecks of pain they left behind do grieve
My very grove. Some memories of moss
I'll keep, for eggs. I know the old routine,
The way the bluebirds come and go. The wing,
Bright blue, the breast, a shade of tangerine,
Belie, alas, the cheep-cheep song they sing.

Hot Spell

This sonnet holds the hope of something hot:
a summer night with soft cicada din,
a sultry rush of fingers on the skin,
a tender lightning bolt that hits the spot.

Or in the city, ripe with heat and rot,
a staircase to a loft where we begin
a strip-down to the hardest core within,
a culture shock, the climax of the plot.

This sonnet drops my hand and doesn't care
that here I lie alone, again, in bed,
the chilly springtime flooding me with pain.
As if I need the sonnet to explain
a couplet rhymes, a couplet is a pair,
my sweat is rain, the heat is in my head.

What We Do

She swallows whole the sun and moon
    and eats my tiny star,
I lead her to my lonely room
    to see what day we are.

Her cosmic arms envelop me,
    her gamma rays caress,
Her hair uncurls my twisted key,
    her seabird screeches yes.

She calls me summer blossom time,
    I call her darling snow,
She sucks me like a lemon-lime
    while icy billows blow.

Red Kiss

Who will miss me when I'm dead?
Maybe someone reading this
is just the sort of daisy head
who will miss me when I'm dead
and planted in a tulip bed.
To her, I offer this red kiss.
Who will miss me when I'm dead?
Maybe someone reading this.

Had We But

The fantasy of me and you in bed—
iambic lines the couplet screw in bed.

Suppose you walk me to the SoHo stop,
drawn to the thought of someone new in bed?

You ride me on your motorbike in Portsmouth—
Charybdis close, a dirty blue in bed.

The common moon in darklit summer bliss,
deserted field the French taboo in bed.

I didn't wake you for the falling stars—
how could I know what you would do in bed?

I sketch you naked sleeping in first light,
the memory of nights for two in bed.

Some airy breaths I bring you here to see—
you bring me here, long overdue in bed.

June

Where is the girl of June who skipped and ran
along the feather lane of birdy hill?
I'd like to give her my last daffodil.
She's lost on river road where she began.

Ladies in Waiting

Again, the ladies in the store,
standing behind me with a smile,
will wait but want a little more.

They want to chat, perhaps explore
my fuzzy cobalt jacket pile.
Again, the ladies in the store

will want to pat my shoulder or,
enchanted by my T-shirt style,
will wait but want a little more,

will slip their fingers past the door
to check the label. Versatile!
Again, the ladies in the store

will add amusement to the chore
of shopping up and down the aisle,
will wait but want a little more

of me, it seems, and my rapport.
I'll wait with them a little while.
Again, the ladies in the store
will wait but want a little more.

What rhymes with breasts?

It's good to know what rhymes with breasts
I wish I'd never seen your breasts

You never know when lines will dance
In girlie pictures in your book

The pirouette of words suggests
My longing for you never rests

It's good to know what rhymes with breasts
I wish I'd never seen your breasts!

While cruising on poetic quests
But it's too late for weak protests

While balancing on cliffs and chance
You stripped. I burned. You gave. I took.

It's good to know what rhymes with breasts
I wish I'd never seen your breasts

You never know when lines will dance
In girlie pictures in your book

may the women in prison dance

women dance, your dresses of purple linen
swaying, dance on flowering grasses, sunlight
dancing too on brown skin and silver bracelets
        you are invited

ice-cold water, clean and refreshing, drink it
lunch is ready, feast on the grapes you gathered,
ripe and juicy, sunflower seeds and almonds,
        roasted and crunchy

lovely island, dreaming of lesbos, scented
seaside song, her laughter is pleasure, shadows
lead the way to late afternoon and making
        love with your lover

Girlhood

In my girlhood
I did my time under a gray
sweatshirt hood.

In a crazy way
I was always alone
in bad neighborhoods.

I used a pay phone
to call my womanhood.
No answer—no good.

Inside I'm this way:
hooded, good,
off the hook.

How Like You This

Lily, dear heart, how like you this,
the sailing of some sweet perfume
and in its wake her salty kiss?

Blithely skirting the abyss,
you climb the staircase to her room.
Lily, dear heart, how like you this,

the summer's fading roar and hiss,
the cool clean cot, the steady zoom,
and in its wake her salty kiss?

Lip to lip, you cannot miss
the minute parsing of her bloom.
Lily, dear heart, how like you this,

the study of a woman's bliss,
the stripping of her prison gloom,
and in its wake her salty kiss?

She studies so as not to miss
the sight of Lily at her loom.
Lily, dear heart, how like you this,
and in its wake her salty kiss?

A Garland of Sighs

A cat?
or moaning cow?
or loon booming the lake?
Some creature howls away our hushed
        hello.
Pleasure
the piney woods
rustles my leafy dreams.
I sleep in shadow bright stained glass
        without her.
Should I
arrange the sheet
around my slumbering
in case the shrieking leaping sheep
        feel shy?
I lost
the key of C
but she was there in spirit
the sharpest note of ecstasy
        was shared.
A car
veers off the street
strikes like a bowling ball.
Manhattan held her shroud and kissed
        her mouth.
A cat
the piney woods
around my slumbering
the sharpest note of ecstasy
        her mouth.

Sonneglige

O négligée neglected far too long.
O fantasies.
O dust. O right and wrong.
O season of heat. O freeze.

Gaze

And oh the amazonian old girl,
her polo collar straight up, and her eyes
averted from the inner-outer whirl
of actions indisputably unwise.
Administration, I believe? So clean,
her clothes, so crisp. An early seventies
collegiate scene, we cross the campus green,
and as we pass, I see her skin say *please*.
I'm sorry there's no language round her lips.
Her walking on suggests that she'd prefer
to stay alone. Now fearful winter tips
my fancy back in time, I fancy her,
the model of restraint, the employee,
who'd never touch young lesbians like me.

World

Anyone could, for love, traverse the world.
Cally sings to trees, disperse the world.

She bikes through forests in a foreign land,
winter, summer, empty purse, the world.

The jet plane lifts and lowers, glints of steel.
The four winds faster, harder, curse the world.

When moss and violets line the rocky creeks,
when all that flows is breaking, verse the world.

Flying or stopping still to pen the page,
having for better or for worse, the world.

My simple summary, my gift to Cally:
there is a good that will reverse the world.

July

July, come find me in the fish's gill.
July, come splash and tip my quick canoe.
July, come whisper who is kind and true.
July, come when you willow, if you will.

The Romance of Middle Age

Now that I'm fifty, let me take my showers
at night, no light, eyes closed. And let me swim
in cover-ups. My skin's tattooed with hours
and days and decades, head to foot, and slim
is just a faded photograph. It's strange
how people look away who once would look.
I didn't know I'd undergo this change
and be the unseen cover of a book
whose plot, though swift, just keeps on getting thicker.
One reaches for the pleasures of the mind
and heart to counteract the loss of quicker
knowledge. One feels old urgencies unwind,
although I still pluck chin hairs with a tweezer,
in case I might attract another geezer.

Lingua Lesbian

The summer English is forbidden,
we have no words to share,
and so a language that was hidden
finds the open air.

Her curls of silky sunny light,
blond blooming in my hand,
entangle me and turn the night
gentle where we stand.

Her Russian babbles in my ear,
mon français sways her hips,
we laugh, go quiet, I draw near
and kiss her rosy lips.

Eureka Springs

The farmer's market in the little Arkansas tourist town, each farmer's tarp tight over a table at the butt-end of a pick-up; and the strawberry farmer in the spring, now the potato farmer in the hotter months, his old face pockmarked and mealy, his teeth large and brown; the farmer from France, with the most popular organic produce, his sensuous accent surreal among the flat patois of the mountain folk, his buttery lettuce light, crisp, tender; Bunny, with her carrots and New England roots, her garlic first green, then moist, pearly cloves, with her bright bags of kale and chard, her bent fingers, her hunger and faded memories; the sky hot baked blue, or dove gray heavy with rain; the banjo player and his spoon-playing wife; the lines of children's drawings in primary colors and puffs of wind.

Dance of a Dozen Lovers

April holds the hands of May,
kissing her tender palms and fingers.
Before the blooms of June hold sway,
April holds the hands of May.
Before July brings her bouquet,
before her lover, August, lingers,
April holds the hands of May,
kissing her tender palms and fingers.

October wanders through the rain,
looking for leaves September left.
Shivering past the window pane,
October wanders through the rain.
Spinning November's weather vane,
December fools; and still bereft,
October wanders through the rain,
looking for leaves September left.

Midnight, the lovers turn in sleep,
in separate months and separate beds,
while January makes the leap.
Midnight, the lovers turn in sleep,
while February slides her sleds
to meet her March. And yet, they weep.
Midnight, the lovers turn in sleep,
in separate months and separate beds.

Workshop Romance

I like your verb, I like your noun,
I like how you've got grammar down,
I like the way you get work done,
I like the prizes you have won,
but, darling, can we paint the town,

and will you wear a cosmic crown,
and spangly satin crimson gown
of sheer, resplendent golden sun?
I like your verb, I like your noun,

I like your stature and renown,
I like your smile, I like your frown,
but, darling, must you always shun
my adjectives? Are you a nun?
Am I a silly, sorry clown?
I like your verb! I like your noun!

Farmer's Market

watermelon: I was pretty once in an androgynous way
zucchini: now I am too old to be looked at by anyone
carrots: man or woman
cantaloupe: I shall not reveal my name or age
okra: if you saw me at the farmer's market
tomatoes: I would not be standing behind a table
onions: laden with tomatoes, onions
garlic: I would be carrying brown paper bags
yellow squash: filling them up
basil: I would not be the teenage boy
scallions: holding his father's arm
lettuce: legs strangely twisted
string beans: who walks with more vertical than horizontal
beets: movement, as if each step requires
eggplant: a leap into the air and the most intense concentration
radish: I am able to climb the staircase two steps at a time
sweet pepper: and climb the staircase seventy times
peaches: until sweat drips like blood
blackberries: my legs marble pillars
turnip: my vanity strong as my marble legs so that
parsley: I quickly forget the boy's twisted legs
cucumber: and his pain

I'm still here

I'm still here holding up the sky for you,
bawling this heart-to-heart goodbye for you.

I'm still the child who cooks the stony stew,
the chickadee who learned to fly for you.

She looks so rich, her face so fresh and new—
you're more than friends, I catch her sigh for you.

Do I sound bitter? Am I green or blue?
Don't leave again! Don't make me cry for you!

I send some poems to the *Screw Review*,
I sit around and wait and die for you.

The marvel of my muse is constant, true.
With dedicated lust, I try for you.

August

Downstream in August, down the heron flew,
straight through the secret bower where we stay
in ferny waterfalls, safe from the day,
forgotten as her words, *a fonds perdu.*

Seashore

Walking the shore alone on cliffs or sand,
the constant senseless waves a steady thrum
(the planet's blood, or mine), the wind at hand,
tangling my thoughts. Where does the wind come from?
They bring me here each summer, to the coast.
Aunt Peggy married wealth, but now it's lost.
She belts a number to the Holy Ghost,
her spirit one with His and damn the cost.
The shades of English novels haunt my mind,
as on the shore, a handsome boy walks by
then stops. Is this the shell I meant to find?
I'm still too young to penetrate the lie,
but I will turn away from boys and home,
and trade my seashells for the mermaid's comb.

Who's this coming out of the sun?

Oh baby you hot hot mama. You hot virgin island at noon summertime. Lizard crawl the wall. Old queen lay by the cove watch wavelets roll. Dew by the light of the sun coming up, come your greenery glittering. Open your tent flap, my little scorpion, bite me, bite me. Drink it down, coconut milk. Baby you hot beauty coming out of the sun you swallow me honeydew. Let me scream a little fuck for you, hm, all right, lay down your bright beam glory here fruit flesh. Come from the sun ray sting me.

Vincent Van Go-Gogh

Again it starts, the solid wall of rain,
good for the farmers, good for cows and cash.
Again it stabs, the rolling pin of pain,
the itch, the broken bone, the tender rash,
the worn-out tooth and eye, the final crash.
We pause to listen to the thunder fart,
as lightning's tongue delivers one more lash.
The earth is tearing up my heart, my heart
a pastry on a shelf, a baker's tart.
Again I brush the silence on in blue,
they could be rising crows, but this my art
repairs the yellow clock I left with you.
I left it on the chair beside the bed,
telling the time, rewinding in my head.

To Be Recited By Sappho On The Fourth Plinth In Trafalgar Square

Father Sky, you droop like a used umbrella.
Passersby, attend to this gallant beauty.
Gone, your pigeon riches, no mouldy droppings
pattern the pavement.

Here my holler rings off the stately towers,
bound for Britain's crown. And resounding sweet as
countertenor solos, my vocalizing
douses the globe with

falcons, fountains, blue-crested wenches, lions.
London heart, I measure your pathways always,
perched pontificating, my arms embracing
skylines and honour.

And

Through summer scorch, be like the trees, breathe,
and through the winter's cracking freeze, breathe.

You gather fragments scratched on broken glass,
and poets drowned in seven seas breathe.

You find her locked inside, you open doors,
you lift her off her buckled knees, breathe.

A knife of pain may bend you over double,
but hover, swing from your trapeze, breathe.

You grip your breath too tight, now let it fly
free from its cage, and like the bees, breathe.

Marry your lungs and air, let steel become
a sigh, be like a leafy breeze, breathe.

When I Meet Her By the Seashore

I shall
untwine her time
unravel her travel
undo her mood
unfasten her battens
unmesh her dress
unbutton her bubbles
unleash her fresh.

And then I shall
unwind her behind
uncouple her trouble
unearth her worth
unstaple her paper
unzip her yip
unbuckle her tickle
untuck her lush.

On the Breakwater

One summer night, when wispy moon had set,
and slothful sea lay tranquil, lapping shore,
and stars glittered, the two young women met
and walked with fingertips in touch, unsure
of where to go, and found a place to sit,
remote, and turned their backs on lights and town
to gaze, without a word, at darkness lit,
but hardly, by a thin gold line thrown down
by Venus, with no sound except the sigh
and suck of ripples, and an owl's high shrill
screeching, at times, from hillside trees nearby.
Then one locked arms around her friend, until
she felt the fervor of her clasp could be
in rhythm with the stealthily heaving sea.

September

September's kohl-rimmed eyes at cabaret,
her turtleneck in black, the color wrong.
But will she listen? No, this is her song,
the little room now falling, flows away.

The Great God Pollen

The Great God Pollen comes to earth in fall
with golden promise, I suppose, to plant
some seeds, to grow some trees, to have a ball
with Goddess Wind, I guess. But no, I can't
rejoice in this romance, because my nose
is dripping, eyes are tearing, throat is sore,
and warm and sunny golden days are those
that bring Lord Pollen and his paramour
the closest to destroying inner peace:
I'm in a fury! Pouting, sullen, crying,
because the summer's gone, because the geese
come down from Canada, because they're flying
with Goddess Wind and Great God Pollen. Pity,
I doubt that I'll survive outside the city.

What will I do?

The answer is a room.
There is a bed.

The bed is there for me to lie on.
I go there

yellow leaves already falling
for the sake of lust

though I must
imagine

"you"
my body creaks closes opens moans moves

as it has
other afternoons.

Daylight Losing Time

I dread turning clocks back an hour.
I'm scared of the turning of leaves.
I'm sorry my mood turns so sour.
I dread turning clocks back an hour.
Can I spring up ahead like a flower?
In fall my clock withers and grieves.
I dread turning clocks back an hour.
I'm scared of the turning of leaves.

Lone Poem

Manhattan. Early eighties. Marilyn
is in, in word, in mind, in bed, in air
I barely breathe, invisible, in skin,
as if this is our lesbian affair.
Instead, she's rising as I crack and sink
and roam to Womanbooks, as if to save
Madwoman in the Attic. Dusk like drink
on sidewalks back, four punkheads misbehave.
One grabs my crotch, for what, for laughs? forget
they could have raped me there in Central Park,
for I was mad and cursed their sorry threat
with lip, with will to live, like wild tree bark
on thick and stately trees I wander under,
lost in the star that tore my heart asunder.

Daylilies

Monday
I phone my soul on Monday, fervent girl,
while leafy shadow puppets sway the curtain.
She gives my bednight bliss a deepsweet swirl.
My little moon loves me, of this I'm certain.

Tuesday
In Crooked Crowville, Tuesday's name is fire.
For her, I take the stand to testify
about the furtive spring of my desire
and how I swallow burning sky and sigh.

Wednesday
Slow goddess, may I fondle Wednesday's ass
and screw her bones into the stratosphere?
Slow goddess hands me water in a glass
and answers very slowly, "Not yet, dear."

Thursday
What quiet Thursday knew, she knew by thunder:
the farmer's hand that cupped her written face,
the poet's papers tossed when she goes under,
the table's wooden legs, the pencil case.

Friday
The weight is all on Friday, oh, what must
she do? Silkslip the sticky golden ring,
flashing the flaxen honeymoon of lust,
upon the bluewing of gamete King Ing?

Saturday
"I know a way," says Saturday, "to lay
a dame: obtain a title, trade, or fame."
This wisdom is dispensed on washing day
to peasants making hay in mortal shame.

Sunday
She is the deep, the gleam, the Sunday dance
I dreamed about. She is the shell, the feather,
the leaf I found, when walking about, by chance.
She makes the lilies bright in rainy weather.

Open Sea

Do you ever rendezvous?
Would you meet me in the mist,
the harbor mist, just me and you?
Or do you never rendezvous;
the thought itself is too taboo.
The literary term is tryst,
if you never rendezvous.
But would you meet me in the mist?

Beginning to Dance

Slow sweet music plays and she
Begins to move her hands as we
O yes she whispers this could be
The granite limits passing me
O wrap me round and quarry me
She swims my waters deep and she
Splash she nestles closer dear
Grove she whispers in my ear
The hazel green trees rustling near

Futile the winds

I close my eyes to go to sleep
and search the velvet night
for any comfort I can keep
or any dream invite.

And then I wonder where you are
and if I could be there,
closer to you, or not so far,
or more than just a prayer.

One word is like a world to me.
Please show me how to reach
the other side of fantasy,
the providence of speech.

Serious night, all undone,
and dark more elemental,
there an answer, there is none,
nor kiss, nor kind, nor gentle.

October

I do adore October's blue sarong,
the sliding slits along her whistling hips,
and I would die to kiss her ruby lips
for all the wet and rotting leaf night long.

Lighthouse Keeper

O pitiless mirror
space empty, smile
tested, trite.
I look for a sign,
you ruthlessly reflect
your slick glass
glued to a dusty off-white
bathroom wall. I'll take
your quick dark ride.

O mattress-mistress,
into you I press
draped with duvet
to every curve.
Flat, inert, hard
you take touch here, there,
then listen to my
then ease my down dark
slope to sleep.

O treasure, lover
naked sleeping
in my tiny room
I draw dawn points
your hands the cello.
Years later I
struggle to remember
kiss, voice, first,
please don't be over.

Anchor Hitch

How do I untie the knot of you?
The poets are professors with degrees!
So much to teach! But I am old and blue.
I lag. I drag behind. I stare at trees,
all woven tight with you for decades now,
cooking and cleaning, mending, keeping house,
wondering what my stringent Fates allow.
They bellow belowdecks and make me grouse.
Their white robes billow on a fancy yacht
on oceans I may never see; and yet,
I am well-fed and comfortable, and not
the waif I was. So why be so upset?
Because the goddess of my dreams is where
I'm not. *Fates, let me go! oh wreck me there!*

Time

Why did you leave me all alone this time,
a bitter Himalayan zone this time?

I found the spices dug in Shakespeare's forest.
(Here exeunt players with a groan this time.)

My tears were buried by bedraggled squirrels,
leaping from limb to limb, bemoan this time.

Gold leaves of words were falling helplessly,
your silence ivy overgrown this time.

How was I supposed to curl on nothing?
It was the hardest coldest stone this time.

Sword branches tore my cope on Halloween,
red berry for the bird unknown this time.

I weave together lachrymary lines,
a cloth for you. I am your own this time.

November

November steels herself for this eclipse.
She twirls her silver ring, light wheels to dark.
Shuffle around the closed amusement park.
Take flight before the skygray canvas rips.

The Loser's Lament

The winning wealthy poets, photographed
by Avedon, will fly between their homes,
collecting prizes, teaching classes, staffed
with personal assistants, stuffed with poems
that dribble from their mouths and land in books
that stock the superstores, the most elite
of schools, and shelves of readers with the looks
to share their beds and take a dinner seat.

But I'm a poet of a single table.
I wash my dishes at the kitchen sink.
I have nowhere to go, and so I think
I'll sit and write a poem at the table.
The price I pay for every line I write
is measured by the gods in bloody light.

Intersection

Judith and Olga
kiss at the red
light two lips touch

mommy grunts
tut-tut two lips
twisted wreckage

sixties spring
the flash of red tulips
signals go

so I go
leap from no
into knowing

Enough

Lover, take this burden, fling my name,
lullaby your baby, sing my name.

A pretty hamlet free from ghosts and worry,
no wounded names foreshadowing my name.

My bitter legacy runs barefoot down the road.
The bees of bothered beehives sting my name.

Fame is such an aphrodisiac—
come on, come on, come on, sweet, bling my name.

We'll wake up marvelling that we're together.
You'll say, like it means everything, my name.

The Need for Reading

Your words, your birds, the wish that fills my hands,
thunderous words, bright feathers, flapping birds,
migrate inside me from your thoughtful lands.
How could I live without your birdy words?
They pierce my muffled house with mating calls,
they read themselves in silence late at night,
they are the years that fade away, the walls
of years I climb to reach you in the light
where I can read your words again. You lay
your words in rows of opals, rubies, pearls,
for me to read but never touch. You play
my senses with an overture that twirls
my wits like ballerinas. In your book
of words, you satisfy my every look.

Sonett

Perhaps it's time for me to hide away
And cry without a sound, my head sunk low,
Then dry my weary eyes again that oh
Have never, never had a restful day–

And let my glances wander fitfully
Off in the gray, the distant atmosphere,
Pursuing phantom fortune, here and here,
Sick from the constant scramble hurting me–

Or is it time to fling myself straight down
In desperation, let my wildness show
In flaming eyes, the gutter of the town

My turf to growl and pant and puff and frown–
Or is it time for me to simply drown
And cry without a sound, my head sunk low.

(after Fradel Shtok's "Sonett")

December

Outside December's window howls the bark
rolled endlessly, big ocean's opal foam,
then silence. Then she thinks of her shalom,
then longs for home, then hears the morning lark.

A Cappella

You take me to the Swan Hotel for drinks,
the Bach cantata still between us, mute.
When you conduct, your hands make slender links
between us: sing crescendo, sing pursuit.

A tiny table sits between us, still,
encircled by a barroom full of noise.
I'm just eighteen, a secret Sapphic thrill
before me: kiss the girls, forget the boys.

You drive me home along the river curve,
the countryside asleep except for light
from dashboard dials, a single flickering nerve
between us: a cappella, ah the night
will hide the way you shift the gears from choir
to this first touch, our holy duet of desire.

You

The night I was entwined in trees,
I tasted you, my tongue alert.
The deer, pathetic in the freeze,
still leapt away, their feelings hurt,
the forest tight. My dreary crumbs
were eaten, but I tasted there,
as if I knew your dainty plums,
the you that isn't only air.

NOTES

"Who leaves me rootless." After Sappho.

"The Stone Insanity." The title is from "Letter to the Front" by Muriel Rukeyser.

"Sea de Sade." "unmoored from the mother ship of culture" is a quote from Camille Paglia.

"Obodowka Cemetery." One of the few facts I know about my mother is that her maiden name is Kittner. With the help of a few German speakers, I translated this poem by Shoah poet, Alfred Kittner (1906-1991). Many thanks to Seree Cohen Zohar, Martin Rocek, Andrés Nader, Adam Elgar, and Roberta Saltzman.

"Arondeus." Willem Arondeus (1894-1943) is a hero of the Dutch Resistance and saved the lives of many Dutch citizens.

"Wu Tsao's Seclusion." Wu Tsao was an early-nineteenth-century Chinese poet. She was unhappily married, wrote erotic poems to courtesans, had women friends and lovers, and spent her last years in seclusion as a Taoist priestess. sappho.com/poetry/wu_tsao.html

"Bee Bouts-rimés." From Wordsworth's sonnet "Hark! 'tis the Thrush, undaunted, undeprest."

"To Elizabeth Bishop." The last line is from Muriel Rukeyser's poem "Looking at Each Other."

"How Like You This." "Dear heart, how like you this?" is from Sir Thomas Wyatt's poem "They Flee From Me."

"Sonneglige." The title is a form invented by Kathrine Varnes which she describes as "a negligent sonnet, that many poets might not even call a sonnet, but one that flirts with a past life, one with a studied disorder."

"Who's this coming out of the sun." The title is from "Under Milk Wood" by Dylan Thomas.

"On the Breakwater." The poem is based on the 1934 short story "Two Hanged Women" by Henry Handel Richardson.

"Futile the winds." The title is from Emily Dickinson's poem, "Wild nights - Wild nights! (269)."

"Sonett." Thanks to Lillian Faderman's help, I translated this sonnet from Yiddish. Fradel Shtok (born in 1888, time of death unknown) was one of the earliest modern Yiddish women writers to gain recognition for her work, and one of the first Yiddish poets to write sonnets.

ACKNOWLEDGMENTS

My thanks to the editors of the following publications, in which some of these poems appeared:

Alimentum Journal: The Literature of Food
American Arts Quarterly
American Journal of Nursing
American Life in Poetry / Poetry Foundation
Amsterdam Quarterly
Angle Journal of Poetry in English
Autumn Sky Poetry
Blue Lyra Review
Bridges: A Jewish Feminist Journal
Chiron Review
Chronicles
Eclectica
Enchanted Conversation
Eyewear
Harrington Lesbian Literary Quarterly
Horizon Review
Journal of Lesbian Studies
Kin Poetry Journal
Light Quarterly
Lilt
Literary Imagination
Measure: A Review of Formal Poetry
Mezzo Cammin
Ms. Magazine Blog
OCHO
Per Contra
Phati'tude Literary Magazine
Poetry Northeast
Rattle
Rhythm Poetry Magazine
Rondeau Roundup
Sentence: A Journal of Prose Poetics
Sinister Wisdom

Sixty-Six: The Journal of Sonnet Studies
SN Review
Snakeskin
Street Spirit
Sugar Mule
The Barefoot Muse
The Brooklyner
The Evansville Review
The Gay & Lesbian Review
The Labletter
The Lyric
The New York Times
The Raintown Review
The Rotary Dial
The Spectator
Tilt-a-Whirl
Verse Wisconsin
Windy City Times Pride Literary Supplement
Writers Among Artists

Anthologies

A Gay & Gray Anthology (New Town Writers Chicago)
Here Come the Brides! Love and Marriage Lesbian-Style (Seal Press)
Hot Sonnets (Entasis Press)
Lady Business (Sibling Rivalry Press)
Measure for Measure: An Anthology of Poetic Meters (Random House)
Obsession: Sestinas in the 21st Century (University Press of New England)
The Bloomsbury Anthology of Jewish American Poetry (Bloomsbury)
The Queer South: LGBT Writers on the American South (Sibling Rivalry)

HEADMISTRESS PRESS BOOKS

Fireworks in the Graveyard - Joy Ladin
Social Dance - Carolyn Boll
The Force of Gratitude - Janice Gould
Spine - Sarah Caulfield
Diatribe from the Library - Farrell Greenwald Brenner
Blind Girl Grunt - Constance Merritt
Acid and Tender - Jen Rouse
Beautiful Machinery - Wendy DeGroat
Odd Mercy - Gail Thomas
The Great Scissor Hunt - Jessica K. Hylton
A Bracelet of Honeybees - Lynn Strongin
Whirlwind @ Lesbos - Risa Denenberg
The Body's Alphabet - Ann Tweedy
First name Barbie last name Doll - Maureen Bocka
Heaven to Me - Abe Louise Young
Sticky - Carter Steinmann
Tiger Laughs When You Push - Ruth Lehrer
Night Ringing - Laura Foley
Paper Cranes - Dinah Dietrich
A Crown of Violets - Renée Vivien tr. Samantha Pious
On Loving a Saudi Girl - Carina Yun
The Burn Poems - Lynn Strongin
I Carry My Mother - Lesléa Newman
Distant Music - Joan Annsfire
The Awful Suicidal Swans - Flower Conroy
Joy Street - Laura Foley
Chiaroscuro Kisses - G.L. Morrison
The Lillian Trilogy - Mary Meriam
Lady of the Moon - Amy Lowell, Lillian Faderman, Mary Meriam
Irresistible Sonnets - ed. Mary Meriam
Lavender Review - ed. Mary Meriam

www.ingramcontent.com/pod-product-compliance
Lightning Source LLC
Chambersburg PA
CBHW050902160426
43194CB00011B/2257